HOW THE U.S. GOVERNMENT WORKS

Written by
Syl Sobel

Illustrated by
Pam Tanzey

BARRON'S

Barron's Educational Series, Inc.

To Marissa,

who asked me to write this book.

All inquiries should be addressed to:
Barron's Educational Series, Inc.
250 Wireless Boulevard
Hauppauge, New York 11788
http://www.barronseduc.com

International Standard Book No. 0-7641-1111-6

Library of Congress Catalog Card No. 99-22328

Library of Congress Cataloging-in-Publication Data

Sobel, Syl.
        How the U.S. government works / written by Syl Sobel ;
illustrated by Pam Tanzey.
        p. cm.
    SUMMARY: Explains the three branches of the federal
government—legislative, executive, and judicial—and how they
work.
        ISBN 0-7641-1111-6
        1. United States—Politics and government Juvenile literature.
    [1. United States—Politics and government.] I. Title.
        JK40 .S66 1999
        320.473—dc21
                                                                    99-22328
                                                                    CIP

Printed in Hong Kong
9 8 7 6 5 4

★ TABLE OF CONTENTS ★

★ INTRODUCTION ★

Why is there a government? To understand this question, first think about your school.

Can you imagine what your school would be like if each class had rules that were different from the rules in other classes? Or if each class had its own schedule that was different from the schedules in other classes?

What would happen if one class wanted to go to the library at 10

o'clock, but another class wanted to use the library at the same time? Who would decide which class would use the library?

And what if the school had no principal, no class parents, no people who worked in the office, and no building custodians? Who would be in charge? Who would help with field trips? Who would keep the building clean?

It would be pretty confusing, wouldn't it?

Well, that's what the United States was like many years ago. Each state had its own rules, but there were no rules for all of the states. Each state had its own type of money, but people couldn't spend the money in all of the states. Georgia had its money, but its money was different from the money in New York. Each state had its own leaders, but no one was the leader of all of the people of all of the states.

The people of the United States decided that this wasn't working. They needed the same rules for everyone. They needed money that everyone could spend. And they needed soldiers and sailors to protect them if people from not-so-friendly countries wanted to fight.

THE PEOPLE OF THE UNITED STATES DECIDED TO FORM A GOVERNMENT TO DO ALL OF THESE THINGS.

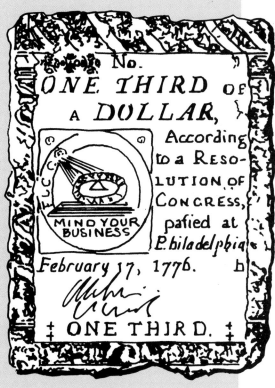

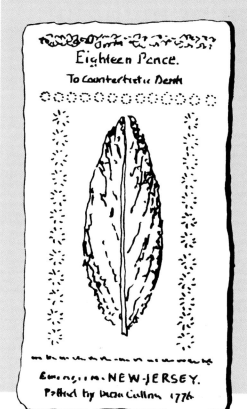

**EACH STATE
HAD ITS OWN
TYPE OF MONEY**

The leaders of the different states got together to create this government. A government is kind of like a business. But it is owned by the people to work for the people. There is a book of rules that tells our government how it is supposed to do its work. It is called the United States Constitution.

The Constitution says that the government has three jobs.

• The first job is to make rules for the United States. These rules are called *laws.*

• The second job is to run the country. This means doing the things that the Constitution and laws of the United States say that the government should do. The government must make sure that the people of the United States obey the laws, too. Running the country also means commanding the army, navy, and air force. And it means working with other countries and meeting with their leaders. It also means doing the many jobs that people want the government to do, such as: deciding what kind of money everyone will use; taking care of land the government owns; helping to build highways and bridges; and helping to keep our food, water, and air clean and safe.

• The third job has several parts: settling arguments when people disagree; deciding what a law means; and deciding whether people who are blamed for not obeying the law must be punished.

So the Constitution divides the government into three parts called *branches.* Each branch has a different job to do.

We the People of the

nsure domestic Tranquility, provide for the common defence and our Posterity, do ordain and establish this Constitution

Article. 1.

Section. 1. All legislative powers herein granted shall be ves of Representatives

Section. 2. The House of Representatives shall be composed of in each State have the Qualifications requisite for Electors of the mo

No Person shall be a Representative who shall not have a and who shall not, when elected be an Inhabitant of that State in whic

Representatives and direct Taxes shall be apportioned among Numbers, which shall be determined by adding to the whole Numbers not taxed, three fifths of all other Persons The actual Enumeration and within every subsequent Term of ten Years in such Manner as thirty Thousand, but each State shall have at least one Representative entitled to chuse three, Massachusetts eight, Rhode Island and eight, Delaware one, Maryland six, Virginia ten, North Carolina

When vacancies happen in the Representation from any

The House of Representatives shall chuse their Speaker and Section 3 The Senate of the United States shall be composed of Senators shall have one Vote.

Immediately after they shall be assembled in Consequence of the Senators of the first Class shall be vacated at the Expiration of Class at the Expiration of the sixth Year, so that one third may be chose

---

1. THE LEGISLATIVE BRANCH

The first branch of the U.S. government is the legislative branch, which makes the laws. This branch is called Congress.

2. THE EXECUTIVE BRANCH

The second branch of the government is the executive branch. The leader of this branch is the president of the United States. The president makes

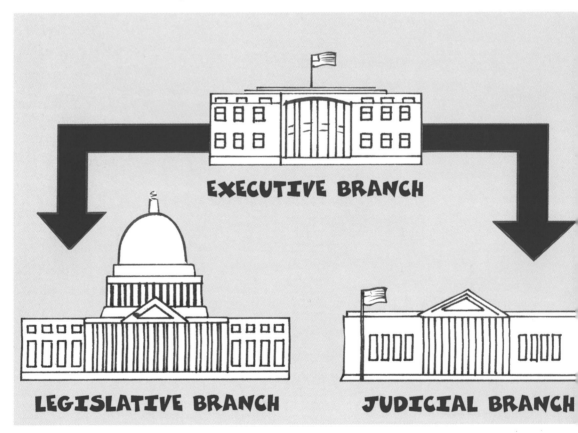

EXECUTIVE BRANCH

LEGISLATIVE BRANCH

JUDICIAL BRANCH

sure that the government performs its jobs according to the laws that Congress makes. The president also commands the army, navy, and air force, and meets with leaders of other countries.

3. THE JUDICIAL BRANCH

The third branch of the government is the judicial branch. It contains the courts. The courts decide how to punish people who do not obey the laws. The courts also settle arguments that people cannot settle themselves.

One confusing thing about the United States is that the whole country has a government, but each state also has its own government. Each state also has its own laws. Sometimes the state laws are very similar to the laws of the United States. But the U.S. government works for all of the people of all of the states. And the laws that the U.S. Congress makes apply to everyone in every state. The laws that each state makes only apply to people who are in that state.

Let's look more closely at the people who work in each branch of the U.S. government.

The Congress makes the laws of the United States. The laws tell the people what they can do and what they cannot do. Some laws protect us from crimes, for example, by saying it is against the law for people to steal money from a bank. Other laws protect our health by telling people who produce food how to make that food clean and safe to eat.

The Congress has two groups, the U.S. Senate and the U.S. House of Representatives.

The people of the United States who are 18 or older choose men and women to be in Congress. This is called *voting* or *electing.* A system of government in which people elect other people to make laws is called a *democracy.*

The members of the House of Representatives do their jobs for two years. The senators do their jobs for six years. Then they have to be elected again if they want to continue in their job. Every two years the government holds an election for Congress. At that time, all of the members of the House of Representatives and one third of the members of the Senate are elected.

THE U.S. SENATE

THE U.S. HOUSE OF REPRESENTATIVES

U.S. CAPITOL BUILDING

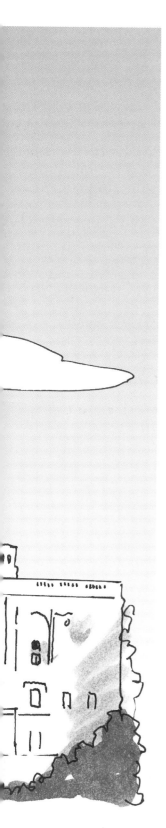

The men and women in Congress meet with each other often. Sometimes all of the senators meet with each other. Sometimes all of the representatives meet with each other. And sometimes senators and representatives meet in smaller groups. These meetings, and most of the work that the Congress does, take place at the U.S. Capitol building in Washington, D.C.

MAKING LAWS

At their meetings, the members of Congress talk about making new laws and changing old laws. These ideas for new laws and changes to old laws are called *bills.* Often, the members do not agree on what a bill should say. This is because they have different ideas about what government should do. When a majority of the senators and a majority of the representatives agree, they send the bill to the president. If the president agrees, then the bill becomes a law of the United States. Sometimes it takes years to make a law. Sometimes laws are made in just a few days.

Some of the most important laws that Congress makes are about money. The government spends money to do its jobs. The government gets the money it needs from the people who live in the United States. The money that people pay to the government is called *taxes.* Congress decides how much taxes the government can collect from the people. These taxes pay for the work of the U.S. government. Congress also makes laws that say when people have to pay taxes to

the government and how much to pay.

For example, some taxes are collected from the money that people earn. A person who earns money for doing a job must give some of that money to the government in taxes. Usually, the more money people make, the more money they must give to the government in taxes.

TAXES PAY FOR GOVERNMENT JOBS

The U.S. government collects taxes so it can pay for things the country needs. For example, taxes help to pay for highways and bridges. U.S. taxes pay for uniforms, ships, and airplanes for the army, navy, and air force. Some of the taxes help people who do not have much money to buy things like food and medicine, and to pay for a place to live. Taxes also help to pay for doctors and scientists to discover new medicines. These medicines can

keep people from getting sick and make them better when they get sick. And, of course, taxes pay the people who work for the government—this includes the president and the members of the Congress. (State and local governments, like counties and towns, also collect taxes. These taxes pay for libraries, schools, teachers, and police officers, for example.)

he Congress spends much of its time deciding how much money the U.S. government can spend. The Congress also decides how much it can collect in taxes. The men and women in Congress know that people need money to buy things for themselves and their families. People therefore do not want to pay too much in taxes. However, people do want the government to do many jobs, and paying for that work costs money. Deciding how much to spend and how much to collect may be the most important work of the Congress. Before citizens vote for members of Congress, they consider many things. People often vote for the person whose ideas they agree with most. Many of these ideas are about how much taxes the government should collect and how much money it should spend.

The executive branch is responsible for spending the government's money the way the Congress says it should be spent. This branch must also make sure that the people of the United States follow the laws that Congress makes. The president is the leader of this branch of the government and is sometimes called the chief executive.

Many people work in the executive branch of the U.S. government. Some people enforce the laws that Congress makes. To *enforce* means to make sure people obey the laws. For example, some members of the executive branch make sure that people pay their taxes. Other people inspect airplanes and factories and make sure they are safe according to the laws that Congress makes. Some executive branch workers inspect the food sold in stores to make sure it is safe to eat. They also inspect the water we drink and air we breathe to make sure it is safe. Other people have the job of making sure that people obey the laws Congress has made about guns, explosives, and drugs. Some people do not obey certain laws, called criminal laws. When this happens, some executive branch workers are responsible for arresting them and putting them in jail.

OLD FAITHFUL

YELLOWSTONE

G·R·A·N·D C·A·N·Y·O·N

Mt. Rushmore

Other people who work for the executive branch help the government do things for the people of the United States. Some help to build highways and bridges. Some take care of the national parks and memorials, like Yellowstone Park and Mount Rushmore, and help visitors learn how to enjoy them safely. Some executive branch workers help farmers learn how to produce more food. Some doctors and scientists also work for the executive branch. They try to discover medicines, or learn more about outer space. And some of the people who work for the executive branch help people in this country who do not have much money. They do this by helping them to get food or a place to live, or helping them to find jobs.

The president has two other important jobs. One is to be in charge of all of the soldiers, sailors, and fliers in the army, navy, and air force. Together, all these groups are called *the military.* Many people work in the military. Some of these people buy and take care of equipment like tanks and planes. Others take care of the military bases where the soldiers, sailors, and fliers live and work. Some people in the military are doctors, some are teachers, some are cooks. The president can order the military to defend the United States at any time. Therefore, all of these people must be prepared to travel anywhere in the world if the president orders them to go.

The president's other important job is to talk with leaders of other countries. They find ways for our country and theirs to work together and get along. Sometimes, our country helps other countries that need money, food, or equipment. Sometimes, the United States helps countries that need military protection from other countries.

The president sometimes meets directly with leaders of other countries. Other times people who work for the president meet with people who work for the leaders of other countries. Some countries want to be friendly. Some do not. Working with other countries and meeting with their leaders is important for the protection of the United States.

If we help other countries, they will usually want to be our friends. But if a country threatens us, the president and people who work for the president tell that country's leaders to stop. The president has the military ready to protect us.

he president can also help to make laws. For example, each year the president gives Congress a plan for how the government should spend its money. The Congress examines the plan and decides how much of it to make into law and how much of it to change.

The president may also have ideas for new laws. These laws may be tax laws, laws about safety, and other ways the government can help the people of this country. The president asks Congress to agree to these ideas so they can become laws. Usually, Congress agrees with some of

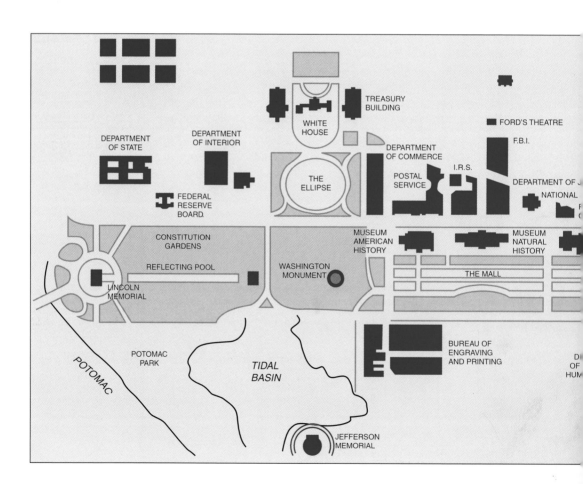

the president's ideas, but not with all of them.

Like the members of Congress, the president is elected. Every four years, the citizens of the United States choose who they want to be president. These people must be 18 or older to vote. The first president of the United States was George Washington. Another famous president was Abraham Lincoln. Do you know who the president is now?

THE CAPITOL AND THE CAPITAL

The president and the president's family live in Washington, D.C., in a building called the White House. The White House is not too far from the

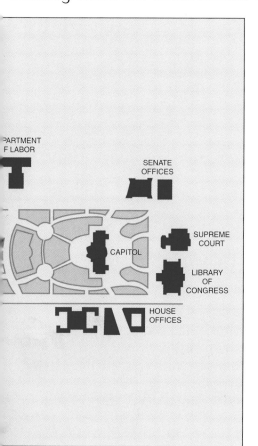

U.S. Capitol, where the Congress works. Many of the people who work for the U.S. government work in buildings in and near Washington, D.C.

Because the leaders of the government are in Washington, D.C., it is called the capital of the United States. If you go to Washington, D.C., you will see lots of buildings where the people in the U.S. government work.

The courts of the United States are called the judicial branch. This is the third branch of the U.S. government. There are also state and local courts in addition to the U.S. courts. Courts are where people go when they have disagreements about the law.

For example, sometimes people disagree with the government about what a law means. A person may think a tax law or a safety law means one thing. But the government says the law means something else. The people and the government go to court, and the court decides what the law means.

Sometimes people hurt each other, or damage someone else's property, or break their agreements. The people go to court, and the court decides who is right and who is wrong. The court also decides whether someone has to pay money for the injury or damage they have caused.

And sometimes the government believes that someone has not obeyed the law. The government brings the person to court. The court then decides whether or not that person has broken the law. If the court finds that the person is guilty, the court also decides how to punish the person.

The people who are in charge of the courts are called judges. Sometimes judges decide by themselves who is right and who is wrong. But sometimes a group of citizens of the United States help the courts make these decisions. These groups of people are called juries.

Judges of the U.S. courts are not elected, although judges of many state courts are. The president picks men and women to become the judges of the U.S. courts. Usually, people who are selected to be judges have had special training. They usually spend many years studying and working with the laws of the United States. The Senate must agree to the president's pick before a person can become a U.S. judge.

Sometimes people do not like the decision of a U.S. judge, called a district judge. When this happens, they can go to a second court of U.S. judges. This second court, called a court of appeals, decides whether the first judge made the right decision. Sometimes, people can even ask a third court to decide if the first two courts made the right decision. This last court is called the Supreme Court of the United States. The Supreme Court is in Washington, D.C. It is right across the street from the U.S. Capitol where Congress works.

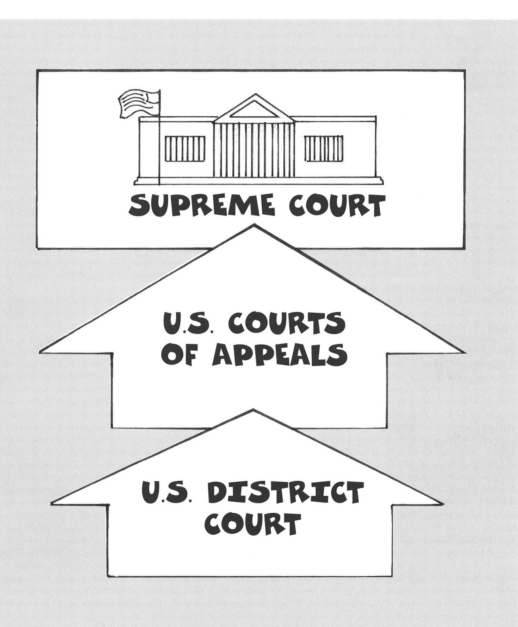

SUPREME COURT

U.S. COURTS OF APPEALS

U.S. DISTRICT COURT

You have learned many things about how the U.S. government works.

You have learned that the U.S. Constitution says how the government should work. And the Constitution says there are three branches of the government. They are:

1. The legislative branch, called the Congress, which makes the laws.

2. The executive branch, led by the president. This branch makes sure that the government and the people follow the laws that Congress makes. The president leads the soldiers, sailors, and fliers. The president also works with leaders of other countries to protect our country and its people.

3. The judicial branch, which is made up of the courts. The courts decide what the laws mean. They also settle arguments between

people. And they decide whether or not people have obeyed the laws and how to punish people who have not.

You have learned that citizens choose the members of Congress and the president by voting. The president chooses the judges of the U.S. courts. Some of the people in Congress, called the senators, have to authorize the president's choice.

You have learned that people pay taxes so the government has money to do its many jobs. You have also learned that many people work for the government.

You now know that Washington, D.C., is the U.S. capital. This is where the leaders of the government and many of the people who work for it are.

There is one very important reason why the U.S. government works. It is the people of the United States. They do many important jobs to keep the government working.

The people vote to choose the leaders of the United States.

The people pay taxes to pay for the work the government does.

The people serve in the army, navy, and air force to help protect the country.

The people tell their leaders what kinds of laws they want. They also tell them what kinds of things the government can do to help the people. People do this by writing letters to their leaders. People also have meetings and gather together in large groups to tell their leaders what they want.

All of the people of the United States help the government do its job. A government in which the people elect leaders and tell them what kind of laws they want is called a democracy.

AND THAT'S HOW THE U.S. GOVERNMENT WORKS.

BILLS

Bills are ideas for new laws and changes to old laws. When a majority of the senators and a majority of the representatives agree on a bill, they send the bill to the president. If the president agrees, then the bill becomes a law of the United States.

CAPITAL OF THE UNITED STATES

Washington, D.C. is called the capital of the United States. This is because the leaders of the government are in Washington, D.C.

CHIEF EXECUTIVE

This is another name for the president of the United States.

CITIZEN

A citizen of a country or town is someone who lives in that country or town. That person has the right to be protected by the government of that country or town. That person also has other rights and certain duties. For example, a citizen of the United States has the right to vote in an election. That citizen also has a duty to pay taxes.

CONGRESS

Congress is the group of people who make the laws of the United States. The U.S. Congress has two groups. They are called the House of Representatives and the Senate. The Congress makes up the legislative branch.

COURTS

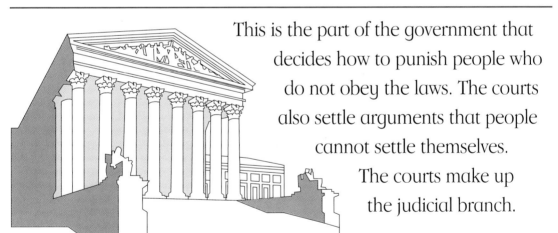

This is the part of the government that decides how to punish people who do not obey the laws. The courts also settle arguments that people cannot settle themselves. The courts make up the judicial branch.

DEMOCRACY

A democracy is a system of government. In a democracy, people elect other people to make laws and to lead the country.

ELECTION

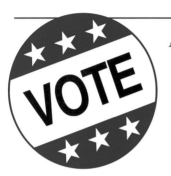

An election is how the people of the United States choose their leaders. The people who are 18 or older vote for members of Congress and for president, for example.

EXECUTIVE BRANCH

The executive branch of the government is responsible for many things. It carries out the laws that Congress makes and makes sure the people obey the laws. This branch also does many jobs for the country. It builds roads and makes sure that the water we drink is safe and the air is clean. The leader of this branch is the president of the United States.

GOVERNMENT

A government is the people and groups who make the rules for the country. It also makes sure people follow the rules. The U.S. government is made up of three branches: the legislative branch, the executive branch, and the judicial branch.

JUDGES

Judges are the people who are in charge of the courts. Judges of the U.S. courts are not elected, although judges of many state courts are. The president picks men and women to become the judges of the U.S. courts. The Senate must agree to the president's pick before a person can become a U.S. judge.

JUDICIAL BRANCH

The judicial branch of the government contains the courts. The courts decide how to punish people who do not obey the laws. The courts also settle arguments that people cannot settle themselves.

LAWS

Laws are the rules that the U.S. Congress makes and the president agrees to. Laws tell the government and the people what they can and cannot do.

LEGISLATIVE BRANCH

The legislative branch of the government makes the laws. The legislative branch of the U.S. government is called the U.S. Congress.

MILITARY

The military is made up of the army, navy, and air force. The military is always ready to protect the United States. The Department of Defense is in charge of the military. Its offices are in a building called the Pentagon.

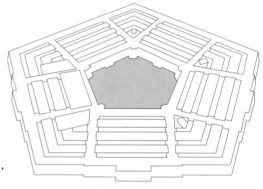

The Pentagon

PRESIDENT

The president is the leader of the executive branch of the government. The president also commands the army, navy, and air force, and meets with leaders of other countries.

The president works in the Oval Office

SUPREME COURT OF THE UNITED STATES

The Supreme Court can decide whether other courts made the right decision. It is located in Washington, D.C.

TAXES

Taxes are the money that people pay to the government. Taxes are used to buy things for the country and pay people to do jobs for the country.

U.S. CAPITOL

The U.S. Capitol is the building in Washington, D.C., where the Congress meets and does most of its work.

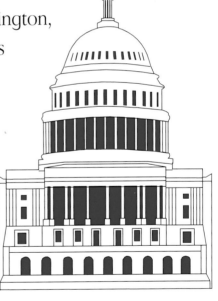

U.S. CONSTITUTION

The U.S. Constitution is made up of the rules that create the U.S. government. It tells the government how it is supposed to operate.

U.S. COURTS OF APPEALS

The U.S. courts of appeals are the second level of the court system in the United States. When people do not like the decision of a judge in the district court, they sometimes go to this second court of U.S. judges.

U.S. DISTRICT COURT

The U.S. district court is the first level of courts in the court system in the United States. People who disagree with each other may go to court so that the court can decide who is right and who is wrong.

U.S. HOUSE OF REPRESENTATIVES

The U.S. House of Representatives is one of the two groups that make up Congress. The members of the House of Representatives are each elected to do their jobs for two years.

U.S. SENATE

The U.S. Senate is one of the two groups that make up Congress. The senators are each elected to do their jobs for six years.

WASHINGTON, D.C.

Washington, D.C., is the capital of the United States. It is the city where the Congress, the president, and the Supreme Court are located. Many of the people who work for the U.S. government work in buildings in and near Washington, D.C.

WHITE HOUSE

The White House is in Washington, D.C. This is the building in which the president and the president's family live.

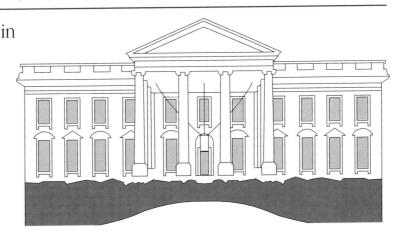

★ INDEX ★

G

Government, 38
  branches, 8, 10–11, 32
    executive, 10–11, 20–27, 32, 38
    judicial, 11, 28–31, 33, 39
    legislative, 10, 32, 40
  creation, 8
  jobs, 8
  purpose, 4–7
  spending, 17, 19, 26
  state, 11
Grand Canyon, 22

H

Health and Human Services, Department of, 21
Highways, building, 8, 17, 23
House of Representatives, 12–13, 37, 42
  offices, 27

I

I.R.S. (Internal Revenue Service) 26

J

Jefferson Memorial, 26
Judges, 30, 39
  district, 30
  selection, 39
Judicial branch, 11, 28–31, 33, 39
Juries, 30
Justice, Department of, 21, 26

L

Laws, 8, 39
  enforcing, 8, 20–21
  making, 12, 15–16, 26–27, 32
  meaning, 28
  See also: Bill
Legislative branch, 10, 32, 40
Library of Congress, 27